Sammy and the Terrible Storm

M. Colleen VonDeBur

ISBN 978-1-64471-084-5 (Paperback)
ISBN 978-1-64471-085-2 (Digital)

First Edition

Covenant Books, Inc.
11661 Hwy 707
Murrells Inlet, SC 29576
www.covenantbooks.com

This book is dedicated to my sister, Anne, whose catchphrase for any situation was, "It's all good."

It felt like it had been hours since Sammy and her father had left the city.

"Are we there yet?" she asked repeatedly.

Cornfields stretched as far as her eyes could see. Finally, the car turned on an old dirt road. It was bumpy and muddy, and the windshield wipers worked hard to clear the yucky mess off.

In the distance, Grandma's house could be seen, and there in the middle of the door stood Grandma. She was so excited to see the car come down the lane that she threw open the door so hard it slammed against the house. She walked to the edge of the porch, waving her hands, calling, "Sammy! Sammy! Get up here and give me a hug. I am so glad to see you. I have planned so many fun things for us to do."

Sammy ran to Grandma's outstretched arms. They hugged for a long time, swaying from side to side.

"I've been waiting for this day for a long time," said Sammy.

"Me too," said Grandma. "Me too."

As the two turned to enter the house, the wind caught the door and slammed it against the house, startling Sammy. She grabbed tightly to Grandma's arm, using it to shield her from the storm. Thunder could be heard in the distance while lightning stretched across the sky.

"A storm is coming," Grandma said. "But don't worry, it's all good. I promise. It will all be good."

While Grandma led her into the kitchen, Sammy looked back at the clouds and the swaying trees. Nervous butterflies filled her stomach as she thought to herself, "All good? how is it all good?"

"You go put your things in the front room and then come join me," Grandma said. "I've fixed you some chocolate milk and cookies for a snack. Then you can tell me all about your school and friends while I finish.

Sammy walked cautiously into the soft light of the front room. She set her suitcase and stuffed bear on the couch and looked around the room at the pictures of her mommy. She smiled.

Suddenly, a flash of lightning and roar of thunder sent her running to the end of the couch where she sat, clutching her worn brown bear with one hand and resting her head on her knees. Tears ran down her cheeks. "This storm is not good at all," she whispered.

In the kitchen, Grandma was finishing working the silky dough. Her apron was as white as snow and stained with butter and cinnamon. She softly sang a tune as she molded the dough and cut it into rolls.

I love the rain.
I love the rain.
Come and dance with me.
Come and dance with me.
Sing happily
for "All is good."
"All is good."
I love the rain.
I love the rain.
Come, sing and dance with me.

Sammy heard the springs of the old oven door squeak when Grandma opened it. She peeked around the end of the couch to see Grandmas slide three trays of cinnamon roll pans on the oven rack and close the door.

"Well, that's done," Grandma muttered. She wiped her hands on her apron, removing the remains of butter and cinnamon.

"Now, where is my Sammy? Sammy, Sammy, where are you? Are you playing hide-and-seek with me? I wonder where that girl is hiding?" Her eyes scanned the room for the small child. "Now, where could she be? Sammy? Sammy, where are you?"

A soft sniffle came from the corner of the room. Grandma moved slowly over to Grandpa's brown chair. Her eyes quickly fixed on the small child in the corner. Grandma's smile turned to a look of concern.

"What is wrong, honey? Why are you crying?"

Through red, swollen eyes and a tear-stained face, Sammy asked, "How is it all good, Grandma? How is the storm all good? I don't know how the storm is all good when it frightens me so much."

"Come out that corner and sit with me." Grandma sat down first and then pulled Sammy close. She covered their legs with a soft warm blanket. Grandma hugged Sammy and then looked out the window at the storm. There was a smile on her face.

"Do you see that square picture on the wall? That's my sister and me. You see, many years ago, I too was scared of storms. I would often gather my stuffed animals and dolls close and hide behind a door, waiting for the storm to pass. Then one day, my sister saw me sitting, clutching my dolls. She asked me what I was afraid of. For several moments, I just sat there, my head down, and shrugged my shoulders.

THUNDER

My sister sat down on the floor next to me and, in a gentle voice, she shared this explanation with me:

"The loud thunder is the voice of
God, calling for our attention.

The wind's fury that sways the trees and
rattles the windows is God blowing
away the bad in the world.

The rain is like our baptism, making us new
again, giving all of us a fresh start.

The lightning is God reminding us that
He is the light of the world.

The silence that follows is God saying,
'It's all good.'"

"Do you understand now? Grandma asked. "There is really nothing to be afraid of. The storm really is all good." Grandma started to hum a melody, and soon the two were both singing.

I love the rain.
I love the rain.
Come and dance with me.
Come and dance with me.
Sing happily,
For "All is good."
"All is good."
I love the rain.
I love the rain.
Come, sing, and dance with me.

About the Illustrator

Robert Schenkel is a freelance storyboard artist and illustrator with thirty years of experience in television commercials, music videos, TV pilots and episodes, and feature films. He has also been a television producer and head of broadcast for three major New York-based agencies.

About the Author

M. Colleen VonDeBur has been married forty years. She has six children and eleven grandchildren. After forty-two years in a classroom, she retired and is enjoying being Nana. Writing this children's book has always been a dream of hers. She hopes there will be others to come that reflect her life's adventures with family.

Her passion has always been taking care of her family. They are the source and inspiration for this book.